All About Zebras

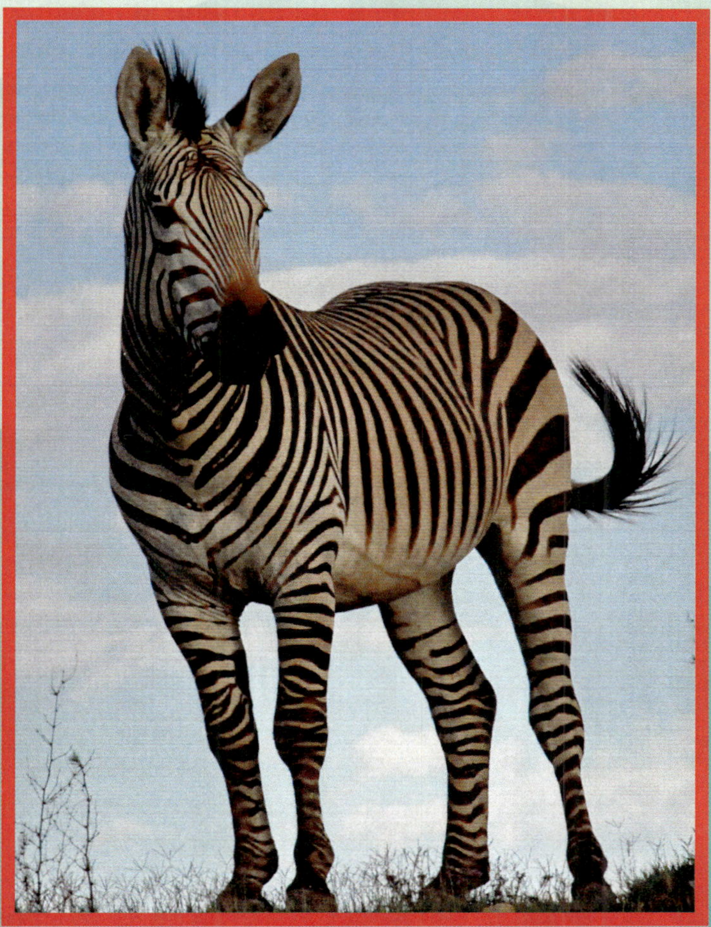

EDventure LEARNING

How to Use This Book

This book is part of our Read Together series, a collection of books designed to be enjoyed by a young reader paired with a more experienced reader, such as a parent, grandparent, or older sibling. Take turns reading out loud together.

 The pages on the left side are meant for the younger reader. These pages use short, simple sentences and larger print. They are marked at the bottom of the page with the symbol shown at left.

The right-side pages are for the older reader. They contain paragraphs with longer sentences and more complex vocabulary. These pages are marked at the bottom of the page with the symbol shown at right.

Shared reading helps new readers gain confidence. It's also a great way for all ages to bond over books. We hope you enjoy this book as you Read Together.

Copyright © 2020 by EDventure Learning LLC

All rights reserved. This book or any portion thereof may not be reproduced or used in any manner whatsoever without the express written permission of the publisher.

Printed in the United States of America
Paperback ISBN: 978-1-64824-020-1

EDventure Learning LLC
5601 State Route 31 #1296
Clay, NY 13039

www.edventurelearning.com
Email us at hello@edventurelearning.com

Table of Contents

What Zebras Look Like .... p. 4

Where Zebras Live .... p. 12

What Zebras Do .... p. 18

Glossary .... p. 28

Index and Credits .... p. 29

What Zebras Look Like

They have stripes.

Zebras are famous for their black and white striped coats. Each zebra has its own unique pattern of stripes. No two are exactly alike. Underneath their fur, zebras have black skin.

Each kind of zebra has different stripes.

plains zebra

There are three types of zebras— plains, Grevy's, and mountain zebras. Plains zebras have wide stripes that wrap all the way around their bellies. Some plains zebras also have lighter gray or brown "shadow stripes" between their main black and white stripes.

Grevy's zebra

mountain zebra

Grevy's zebras have very thin stripes and solid white bellies. Mountain zebras also have solid white bellies, but their stripes are wider than those of Grevy's zebras.

Baby zebras have brown stripes.

foal

When a baby zebra (called a **foal**) is born, its stripes are brown and white. The brown stripes darken to black as the zebra gets older.

They look a lot like horses.

Other than the stripes, zebras look a lot like horses. That's because the two types of animals are very closely related. Like horses, zebras have four thin legs, hooves, a long face, and a mane. Zebras are shorter than horses, however, averaging around 4 feet (1.2 m) tall.

Where Zebras Live

Zebras live in Africa.

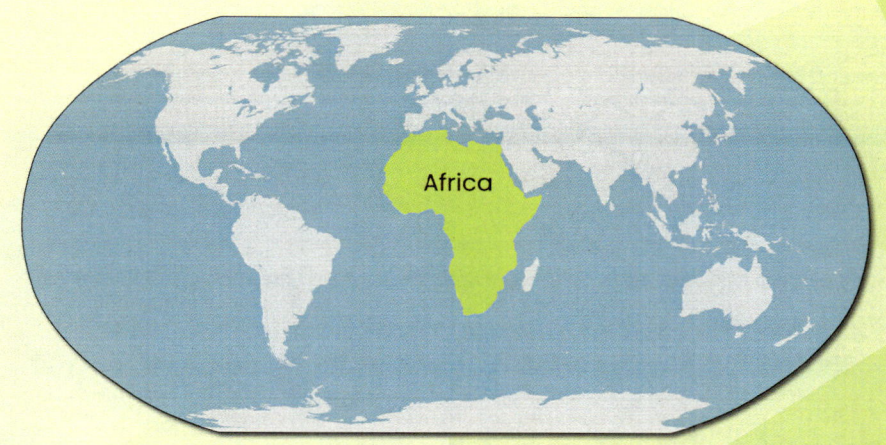

All three types of zebras live in the eastern and southern parts of the continent of Africa.

Most zebras live on plains.

Plains zebras are the most common type of zebra. They, along with Grevy's zebras, live in the **savanna**. The savanna is flat, open land covered in tall grasses and scattered trees.

savanna

Some zebras live on rocky land.

The third type of zebras, mountain zebras, live in mountainous areas in southern Africa.

What Zebras Do

Zebras eat plants.

Zebras are **herbivores** that mostly graze on grass. They also munch on leaves, twigs, and shrubs.

They break off plants with their sharp, strong front teeth and grind them with their large, flat back teeth.

They move in herds.

Zebras live in small family groups. Sometimes, those units join together to form huge **herds**. The herd travels together to find enough grass to eat. They will sometimes even join up with herds of other herbivores. Even when in a herd of hundreds, families of zebras stick close together.

They help each other stay safe.

Zebras have many predators, such as lions, cheetahs, leopards, hyenas, and crocodiles. Zebras work to protect each other. They call out when danger is near, and the strongest males will stay back while the rest of the herd runs away. A zebra's best defense is to run, but if they have to fight, they can use their strong legs to give a fast and powerful kick. A good kick can knock a predator back hard enough to give the zebra a chance to escape.

They bark.

Zebras use many sounds to communicate, including barks, brays, and huffs. They also communicate using body language, such as baring their teeth or flattening their ears.

They are not tame.

Humans have domesticated many of the zebras' relatives, such as horses and donkeys, in order to ride them and use them for work animals. People have not been able to train zebras in the same way, however (though many have tried). Zebras are used to being on the defensive, since they are naturally surrounded by so many predators. This makes them strong-willed, aggressive, and quick to run away. They are not as friendly to humans as their horse relatives.

Glossary

Herbivore
Animal that eats only plants

Herd
Large group of zebras

Foal
Baby zebra

Savanna
Plains with scattered trees and a warm climate

Index

A
Africa, 12-13, 17
Appearance, 4-11, 19

D
Defense, 22-23, 27

F
Foal, 8-9, 28
Food, 18-19, 21

G
Grevy's zebra, 7, 15

H
Habitat, 12-17
Herd, 20-23, 28

M
Mountain zebra, 7, 17

P
Plains zebra, 6-7, 15

S
Savanna, 15, 28

Credits

The images in this book are used with permission as follows. Images not listed here are © EDventure Learning LLC.

Cover and title page: Barbara Fraatz | Pixabay; Interior backgrounds: Kappy Kappy | Rawpixel; p. 3: Mikhail Makeev | Dreamstime; p. 4: Jeff Griffith | Unsplash; p. 5: Fabrizio Frigeni | Unsplash; p. 6: Ruchindra Gunasekara | Unsplash; p. 7: Gabriel Tresch | Unsplash (top), Wolfgang Hasselmann | Unsplash (bottom); p. 8: Vicki Roberts | Pixabay; p. 9: Lady Bugz | Unsplash; p. 10: maja7777 | Pixabay; p. 11: Tiago Almeida | Unsplash (top), Alexander Lesnitsky | Pixabay (bottom left), macrovector | Freepik (bottom right); p. 12: Magda Ehlers | Pexels; p. 13: Clker Free Vector Images | Pixabay (top), Ray Rui | Unsplash (bottom); p. 14: Ron Dauphin | Unsplash; p. 15: Sutirta Budiman | Unsplash; p. 16: Thomas Pedrazzoli | Pixabay; p. 17: Frans Van Heerden | Pexels; p. 18: Barbara Fraatz | Pixabay; p. 19: Fabrizio Frigeni | Unsplash (top), Maarten van den Heuvel | Unsplash (bottom); p. 20: Pawan Sharma | Unsplash; p. 21: Danielle Barnes | Unsplash; p. 22: Avel Chuklanov | Unsplash; p. 23: Magda Ehlers | Pexels (top), dpatdfci | Pixabay (bottom); p. 24: Isabelle Duarte | Pixabay; p. 25: Adriana Gois | Pixabay; p. 26: Skeeze | Pixabay; p. 27: Jonatan Pie | Unsplash; p. 28 (from top): Fabrizio Frigeni | Unsplash, Pawan Sharma | Unsplash, Vicki Roberts | Pixabay, Sutirta Budiman | Unsplash

Check out these other titles in the Read Together series!

All About Camels

All About Cheetahs

All About Giraffes

All About Elephants

All About Kangaroos

Keep in touch!

FOLLOW US ON SOCIAL MEDIA

     @edventurelearning

   www.edventurelearning.com

   Want freebies? Email us at **hello@edventurelearning.com** with the subject "Read Together" to join our newsletter and we'll send you free printables to keep the learning going!

All About Lions

All About Penguins

All About Polar Bears

All About Tigers

All About Zebras

Made in United States
North Haven, CT
12 February 2025